Key Stage 2 LEARN

Materials
& Physical Processes

NAPE
National Association for Primary Education

Contents

AUTHOR: Camilla de la Bédoyère
EDITORIAL: Catherine de la Bédoyère, Quentin de la Bédoyère, John Bolt,
Vicky Garrard, Kate Lawson, Sally MacGill, Julia Rolf, Lyndall Willis
DESIGN: Jen Bishop, Dave Jones, Colin Rudderham, Mike Spender
ILLUSTRATORS: David Benham, Sarah Wimperis
PRODUCTION: Chris Herbert, Claire Walker
Thanks also to Robert Walster

COMMISSIONING EDITOR: Polly Willis
PUBLISHER AND CREATIVE DIRECTOR: Nick Wells

3 book Pack ISBN 1-84451-053-0   Book ISBN 1-84451-035-2
6 book Pack ISBN 1-84451-066-2   Book ISBN 1-84451-083-2
First published in 2003

A copy of the CIP data for this book is available from the British Library
upon request.

Created and produced by
FLAME TREE PUBLISHING
Crabtree Hall,
Crabtree Lane,
Fulham, London SW6 6TY
United Kingdom
www.flametreepublishing.com

Flame Tree Publishing is part of The Foundry Creative Media Co. Ltd.

© The Foundry Creative Media Co. Ltd, 2003

Printed in Croatia

D0620181

Foreword

Sometimes when I am crossing the playground on my way to visit a primary school I pass young children playing at schools. There is always a stern authoritarian little teacher at the front laying down the law to the unruly group of children in the pretend class. This puzzles me a little because the school I am visiting is very far from being like the children's play. Where do they get this Victorian view of what school is like? Perhaps it's handed down from generation to generation through the genes. Certainly they don't get it from their primary school. Teachers today are more often found alongside their pupils, who are learning by actually doing things for themselves, rather than merely listening and obeying instructions.

Busy children, interested and involved in their classroom reflect what we know about how they learn. Of course they learn from teachers but most of all they learn from their experience of life and their life is spent both in and out of school. Indeed, if we compare the impact upon children of even the finest schools and teachers, we find that three or four times as great an impact is made by the reality of children's lives outside the school. That reality has the parent at the all important centre. No adult can have so much impact, for good or ill, as the young child's mother or father.

This book, and others in the series, are founded on the sure belief that the great majority of parents want to help their children grow and learn and that teachers are keen to support them. The days when parents were kept at arm's length from schools are long gone and over the years we have moved well beyond the white line painted on the playground across which no parent must pass without an appointment. Now parents move freely in and out of schools and very often are found in the classrooms backing up the teachers. Both sides of the partnership know how important it is that children should be challenged and stimulated both in and out of school.

Perhaps the most vital part of this book is where parents and children are encouraged to develop activities beyond those offered on the page. The more the children explore and use the ideas and techniques we want them to learn, the more they will make new knowledge of their very own. It's not just getting the right answer, it's growing as a person through gaining skill in action and not only in books. The best way to learn is to live.

I remember reading a story to a group of nine year old boys. The story was about soldiers and of course the boys, bloodthirsty as ever, were hanging on my every word. I came to the word khaki and I asked the group "What colour is khaki?" One boy was quick to answer. "Silver" he said, "It's silver." "Silver? I queried. "Yes," he said with absolute confidence, "silver, my Dad's car key is silver." Now I reckon I'm a pretty good teller of stories to children but when it came down to it, all my dramatic reading of a gripping story gave way immediately to the power of the boy's experience of life. That meant so much more to him, as it does to all children.

JOHN COE
General Secretary
National Association for Primary Education (NAPE).

NAPE was founded 23 years ago with the aim of improving the quality of teaching and learning in primary schools. The association brings together parents and teachers in partnership.

NAPE, Moulton College, Moulton, Northampton, NN3 7RR, Telephone: 01604 647 646 Web: www. nape.org.uk

Materials & Physical Processes is one of six books in the **Learn** series, which has been devised to help you support your child through Key Stage Two.

The National Curriculum gives teachers clear guidelines on what subjects should be studied in Science, and to what level. These guidelines have been used to form the content of both this book and **Living Things**, the first Science text in this series.

Each page contains exercises for your child to complete, an activity they can complete away from the book and **Parents Start Here** boxes to give you extra information and guidance. At the end of the book you will find a checklist of topics – you can use this to mark off each topic as it is mastered.

This book has been designed for children to work through alone; but it is recommended that you read the book first to acquaint yourself with the material it contains. Try to be at hand when your child is working with the book; your input is valuable. The influence science exerts on our society is increasing at an ever greater rate. Sadly, many parents feel that science is something they know little about – this book may help you overcome gaps in your own knowledge and thus be in a better position to teach your child.

Encourage good study habits in your child:

- Try to set aside a short time every day for studying. 10 to 20 minutes a day is plenty. Establish a quiet and comfortable environment for your child to work and provide suitable tools e.g. sharp pencils and good handwriting pens.

- Give your child access to drinking water whenever they work; research suggests this helps them perform better.

- Reward your child; plenty of praise for good work motivates children to succeed.
Ensure your child eats a healthy diet, gets plenty of rest and lots of opportunity to play.

This book is intended to support your child in their school work. Sometimes children find particular topics hard to understand; discuss this with their teacher, who may be able to suggest alternative ways to help your child.

Top Tip!
If your child struggles with anything, don't worry – let them go at their own pace.

Parents Start Here...

Some of the words used in science can be daunting. Encourage the use of a Word Book to record new words and definitions.

Materials

The word material describes what things are made from. Materials may be natural or man-made (synthetic). Natural materials can come from living or non-living sources. Materials can be:

From Living Things
- Wood and paper – come from trees
- Leather – comes from cow skin
- Wool – comes from sheep fur
- Silk – comes from the cocoons of the silk moth
- Cotton – comes from the cotton plant
- Linen – comes from the flax plant
- Mother of Pearl – comes from the insides of shells

Raw materials, wood for example, are normally treated in some way before we use them. Wood is turned into pulp and mixed with chemicals before it becomes paper.

Rocks In The Ground
- Chalk, coal, clay, sand and soil
- Precious gems, such as rubies, diamonds and amethysts
- Metal, such as aluminium, iron, copper, silver and gold

Made By People
- People can take natural materials and turn them into new materials.
- Oil is turned to plastic, sand is made into glass, clay becomes pottery etc.

Chalk, coal and oil were all made millions of years ago, from the bodies of dead animals and plants.

The Properties Of Materials

We describe materials by their properties. These properties make them useful for certain jobs. When you decide what material you will use to do a certain job, you have to think about its properties.

Here are some properties of materials and their opposites.

soft	**hard**
flexible (can be bent)	**rigid** (cannot be bent)
transparent (see-through)	**opaque** (can not be seen through)
waterproof	**absorbent** (soaks up liquid)
floats	**sinks**
rough	**smooth**

Home Learn

Write some properties that describe the following materials. You can use the properties mentioned on this page, or think of different ones.

a) glass _____

b) plastic raincoat _____

c) nappy _____

Activity

Collect old boxes, tubes and packaging and start a 'building box'. Put in some glue, scissors and string. Whenever you are bored you can go to your building box and start inventing.

Check Your Progress!

Materials ☐

Turn to page 48 and put a tick next to what you have just learned.

Top Tip!
Bring what your child learns into everyday life – they'll remember it even better.

Parents Start Here...

There are many practical ways your child can experiment with the properties of materials. Give them the opportunity to test materials for their properties of water resistance, strength, flexibility etc.

Materials And Properties

Glass

- is transparent (you can see through it)
- can be moulded into different shapes while it is being made
- breaks easily   • is waterproof

Think of one reason why it is good that glass is waterproof:

_____

Plastic

- is strong and durable (lasts a long time)
- is waterproof
- can be moulded into different shapes while it is being made
- can be transparent or opaque (you can't see light through it)

Think of one reason why it is good that plastic is strong:

_____

Metal

- is strong and durable   • is waterproof
- is shiny and reflects light   • is opaque
- can be moulded and bent into different shapes

Think of one good reason why it is good that metal is durable:

_____

Fabric
- is soft and quite strong
- can be stretchy
- is not usually waterproof
- is opaque but can be coloured
- can be made into different shapes
- can be cut and sewn

Think of one reason why it is good that fabric can be cut and sewn:

_____

Home Learn

a) Name two materials you might use to make a hammer.

_____

b) Name some of the materials you might find in a car.

_____

c) Name one use of transparent plastic.

_____

Activity

A hundred years ago plastic had not been invented. Find things made of plastic in your home and try to imagine what different materials might have been used to make them instead.

Check Your Progress!
Materials And Properties
Turn to page 48 and put a tick next to what you have just learned.

Top Tip! If your child struggles with anything, don't worry – let them go at their own pace.

Parents Start Here...

Explain to your child how important it is to conduct any experiment in safety.

Conductors And Insulators

Heat

- Heat travels from hot places to cold places until they are both the same temperature. That is why your hot water bottle starts off hot, but by the morning it is the same temperature as your bed.

- Heat travels through all materials, but moves quicker through some materials, like metal, than others, like wood. That is why you can stir a hot sauce with a wooden spoon, but not with a metal spoon.

- Materials that allow heat to move through them easily are called thermal conductors e.g. metal.

- Materials that stop heat moving through them easily are called thermal insulators e.g. wood, trapped air, fabric.

Fabrics are usually good thermal insulators; that's why you wear lots of clothes when it's cold. Clothes made of metal, rather than fabric, would not keep you warm because they would conduct all of your body heat to the outside air.

heat is trapped in   heat travels out

Electricity

- Like heat, electricity can move through materials. Some materials can conduct electricity. They are called electrical conductors. Most metals are electrical conductors.

- Materials that do not conduct electricity are called electrical insulators. Wood, glass and plastic are electrical insulators.

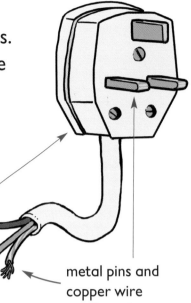

plastic case and plastic cover on wire stop electricity from travelling to your hand

metal pins and copper wire conduct electricity

Caution: electricity can kill you.

Home Learn

Complete these sentences:

1. Stirring a hot sauce with a_____ spoon is a good idea because _____ is a _____ _____.

2. Stirring a hot sauce with a _____ spoon is a bad idea because _____ is a _____ _____.

Activity

Pour some water, from the hot tap, into containers made from different materials (e.g. polystyrene, metal, glass, china) and cover them. Which material keeps the water warm for longest?

Check Your Progress!
Conductors And Insulators
Turn to page 48 and put a tick next to what you have just learned.

Top Tip! If your child loses concentration here, let them take a break.

Parents Start Here...

Let your child help you with cooking; they will be able to observe how solids, such as butter, become liquids when heated.

Solids, Liquids And Gases

A material's state can be described as solid, liquid or gas. Materials are made up of lots of little particles.

Imagine you stuffed one of your socks with loads of building bricks until you couldn't fit any more in. It would look like this:

the sock is rigid and hard – there is no room for movement

This gives you an idea of how the particles are arranged in a solid. Tables, teapots and trains are all made from solid materials.

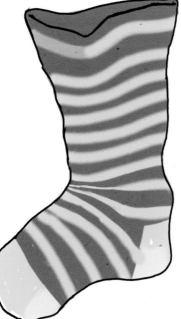

you can change your sock's shape

Now imagine you've emptied out some of those building blocks from your sock.

This gives you an idea of how the particles are arranged in a liquid. The particles are still in the sock, but they have room to move.

Water, milk, blood, oil and orange juice are all liquids. Mercury is a liquid metal.

Now imagine taking the bricks out of the sock and spreading them around the room.

This is how the particles are arranged in a gas. They can move about freely. Air contains lots of gases, like carbon dioxide and oxygen. Helium is also a gas.

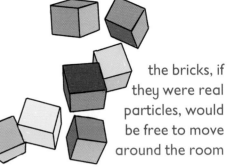

the bricks, if they were real particles, would be free to move around the room

When there are no particles at all, it is a vacuum.

particles are packed tightly together

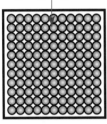

SOLID
solids cannot be squashed and they do not flow

particles are loosely packed

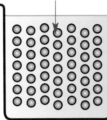

LIQUID
liquids flow and take the shape of the container

particles are free to move

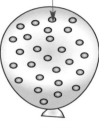

GAS
gases are usually invisible and spread out to fill the container

Home Learn

Are the following materials solid, liquid or gas at normal room temperature?

TRY THIS

Activity

Helium is contained in balloons. Helium is lighter than air. How do we know that?

	Solid	Liquid	Gas
Vinegar			
Oxygen			
Petrol			
Jelly			
Plastic			
Mercury			
Carbon Dioxide			
Paper			
Blood			
Helium			

Check Your Progress!
Solids, Liquids And Gases
Turn to page 48 and put a tick next to what you have just learned.

Top Tip! Don't worry if your child does not understand straightaway – children learn at different speeds.

Parents Start Here...

Set up an experiment with your child where you can prove that when water freezes it expands in size.

Water

Water exists in three states: solid (ice), liquid (water) and gas (steam). This picture shows you what happens to water when you heat it or cool it.

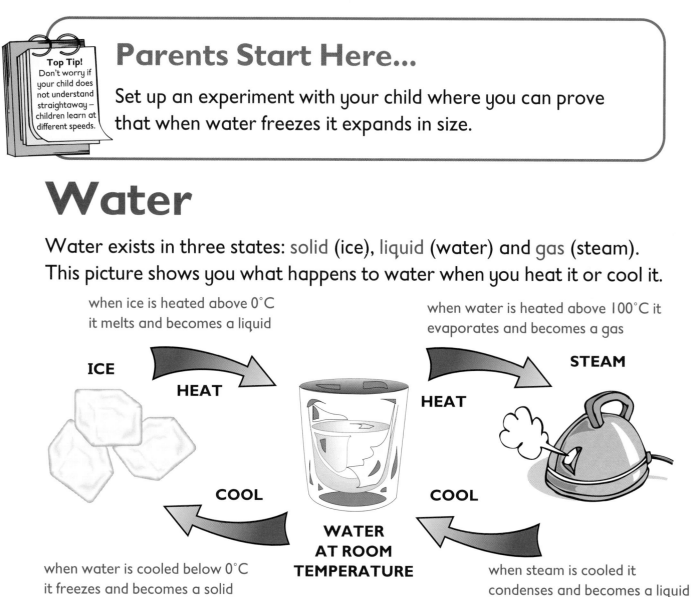

when ice is heated above 0°C it melts and becomes a liquid

when water is heated above 100°C it evaporates and becomes a gas

ICE

HEAT

STEAM

HEAT

COOL

WATER AT ROOM TEMPERATURE

COOL

when water is cooled below 0°C it freezes and becomes a solid

when steam is cooled it condenses and becomes a liquid

There are some long words in this diagram that you need to learn:
Evaporate: turning liquid into a gas. Condense: turning a gas into a liquid.
Melt: turning a solid into a liquid. Freeze: turning a liquid into a solid.

Water in different states has different properties:

Ice
• expands (gets bigger) when it freezes • floats

Liquid Water
• is good for dissolving things • can hang about in the air in tiny droplets.
This is called water vapour. (Clouds and mist contain water vapour.)

Steam
• is invisible and very dangerous because it is hot

The Water Cycle

The changing states of water are reversible. This means that liquid water can become steam and steam can change into liquid water again. This picture shows you how water vapour becomes rain.

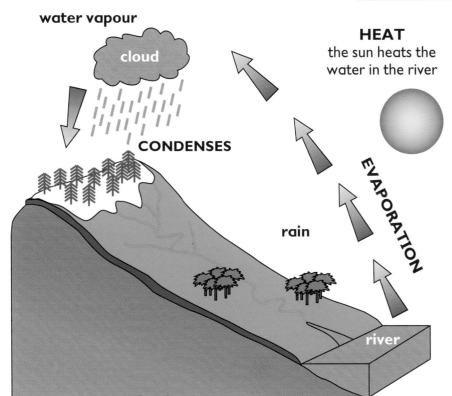

water vapour

cloud

HEAT
the sun heats the water in the river

CONDENSES

EVAPORATION

rain

river

Home Learn

True Or False?

- When water is cooled it evaporates. ☐ True ☐ False
- The particles in steam are further apart than the particles in water. ☐ True ☐ False
- Rain is melted snow falling from the clouds. ☐ True ☐ False
- Ice floats because water expands when it freezes. ☐ True ☐ False

TRY THIS Activity

The next time you have a bath or shower ask yourself how water end ups on the bathroom mirror and window. Think about what the cool glass might do to the water vapour.

Check Your Progress!

Water ☐

Turn to page 48 and put a tick next to what you have just learned.

Parents Start Here...

Top Tip! Go through this page as often as you like until your child understands it fully.

Science can become dull if all you do is read about it. Children love the bits of science they can get involved in; encourage lots of (safe!) experimenting.

Mixing Materials

You might think that sand on the beach is just one material.

If you look closely, you will see that the sand is a mixture of materials. There are stones, shells, bits of bone and sand all mixed together.

Take a handful of soil and look at that closely – you will find bits of rock, water, dead plants, bits of dead bug and, maybe, even a few live ones.

Like sand, soil isn't one single material, but a mixture. Sand and soil are mostly mixtures of different solids. Let's try mixing some materials.

Ask a grown-up before you begin.

Experiment 1: Mixing Two Solids.
Take a cup of sugar and a cup of flour and use a spoon to mix them together in a bowl. You have now mixed two solids and they would not be easy to separate.

Experiment 2: Mixing Two Liquids.
Take a glass of milk and a glass of water and use a spoon to mix them together in a bowl. You have now mixed two liquids, and they would not be easy to separate.

Now half-fill a transparent glass with water and pour a little cooking oil into it. Stir and watch what happens. You will see that the two liquids will not mix. Can you think of some ways you might separate them?

14

Experiment 3: Mixing A Solid And A Liquid.

Pour some salt into half a glass of tap-hot water and stir. The salt is still in the glass, but it has dissolved. You have mixed a solid and a liquid. You will be separating them later, so don't throw this solution away. Pour it into a saucer and leave in a warm place.

Repeat your experiment but use flour instead of salt. Describe what you see.

_____

_____

When a solid dissolves it mixes completely with a liquid.
A solution is a mixture of a liquid and a solid that has been dissolved.
The liquid that does the dissolving is called a solvent.
Solids that do not dissolve are called insoluble.

Home Learn

Complete the sentences:
a) When a solid does not dissolve in water we say it is _____.
b) Water dissolves some solids so we say it is a _____.

Activity

Find out which of these solids completely dissolve in water.
Ask a grown up to help.
Tip: some things don't dissolve in cold water, but do in hot water.
Salt; pepper; mustard; butter; stock cube; tomato ketchup; cooking oil; jelly cubes; sugar; coffee granules; tea leaves.

Check Your Progress!
Mixing Materials
Turn to page 48 and put a tick next to what you have just learned.

Parents Start Here...

Remind your child that dissolved solids have not gone – they are still present in a solution but have become invisible.

Changing And Changing Back

When you were mixing materials you left a solution of salt and water in a warm place. If you have been checking on it you will have noticed that the water has been evaporating, leaving behind powdery white salt crystals.

You have separated the salt from the solution using evaporation. This is possible because dissolving is a reversible process.

We saw that the states of water are reversible when we looked at the water cycle.

There are some processes that are irreversible. This means you can not put things back the way they were.

Concrete is made from a mixture of sand, water, gravel and cement. The mixture causes all the ingredients to change and become hard. You can not turn concrete back into its ingredients.

Heating And Cooling
Heating an egg is an irreversible process. You cannot change the fried egg back into a raw egg.

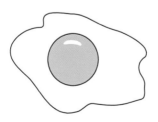

Heating chocolate is a reversible process. Heat melts it, but when it cools down it is still the same, although it might have a different shape.

Heating wood, coal or oil causes them to burn. This gives off energy. We burn fuel like these to give us energy for light, heat and to make our machines work. Burning is an irreversible process.

Home Learn

Complete the table:

	Reversible	Irreversible
Freezing a chicken	✓	
Boiling an egg		
Dissolving sugar in water		
Baking bread		
Melting candle wax		
Grilling bread to make toast		

Activity

Make a solution of salt and water and put in half of an ice tray. Put plain water in the other half. Label the sides. See which side freezes first. Does this tell you why your local council puts salt on the roads in winter?

Check Your Progress!
Changing And Changing Back
Turn to page 48 and put a tick next to what you have just learned.

Top Tip! Bring what your child learns into everyday life – they'll remember it even better.

Parents Start Here...

Investigating the properties of soil is part of the curriculum. Tell your child what sort of soil is found in your locality, and what types of plants grow in it.

Separating

We were able to separate the salt from a solution of salt and water. We can separate other mixtures too.

Separating Solids From Water

Experiment 1: Offer to help a grown-up cook some peas and sweetcorn in water. When the vegetables are cooked, watch the grown-up pour the mixture through a sieve or colander. You will notice the water goes into the sink and the vegetables stay behind. They have been separated.

Experiment 2: You can separate a solid that has dissolved using the evaporation method (remember the salt and water?).

Separating Solid From Solid

Experiment 3: Easy! You can separate the peas from the sweetcorn. It may be boring, but you separate these two solids using your fingers. It's not always so easy. Supposing you had to separate a mixture of flour and salt.

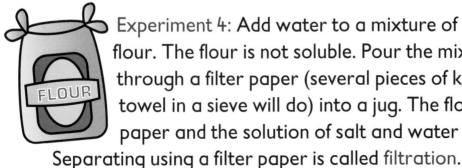

Experiment 4: Add water to a mixture of salt and flour. The flour is not soluble. Pour the mixture through a filter paper (several pieces of kitchen towel in a sieve will do) into a jug. The flour will stay in the paper and the solution of salt and water will be in the jug. Separating using a filter paper is called filtration.

How will you separate the salt from the water?

_____

_____

_____

Sometimes it is impossible to separate two solids. This used to be two balls of Plasticine. How could we ever separate them?

Home Learn

Sand is insoluble. Describe how you would separate a mixture of sand and water:

_____

_____

_____

Activity

TRY THIS

Ask a grown-up if you can get mucky in the garden or the park. Dig up some soil and put it in a bucket of water. Stir and watch what happens to the water.

Check Your Progress!

Separating ☐

Turn to page 48 and put a tick next to what you have just learned.

Quiz

On Your Marks. In each round, award yourself marks for correct answers. You are allowed to look back through the book for some help.

For ⭐ ⭐ ⭐ get all 4 answers right

For ⭐ ⭐ get 3 answers right

For ⭐ get 1 or 2 answers right

Colour in your total star score at the end of the quiz.

Round One

a) Which of these materials is a thermal insulator?
- ☐ silver
- ☐ gold
- ☐ wool
- ☐ steel

b) Which of these materials is an electrical conductor?
- ☐ cotton
- ☐ metal
- ☐ paper
- ☐ glass

c) Which of these materials is transparent?
- ☐ polythene
- ☐ polystyrene
- ☐ wool
- ☐ aluminium

d) Which material is shiny?
- ☐ stainless steel
- ☐ linen
- ☐ polystyrene
- ☐ wool

Round Two

a) Which of these materials is a gas at room temperature?
- ☐ helium
- ☐ milk
- ☐ blood
- ☐ wood

b) Which of these materials is a liquid at room temperature?
- ☐ coal
- ☐ glass
- ☐ oil
- ☐ gold

c) Which of these materials is a solid at room temperature?
- ☐ carbon dioxide
- ☐ water
- ☐ oxygen
- ☐ coal

d) Which of these materials becomes a gas at 100°C?
- ☐ oil
- ☐ helium
- ☐ water
- ☐ petrol

Round Three

a) When liquid water evaporates it becomes:
- ☐ ice
- ☐ condensation
- ☐ boiled
- ☐ water vapour

b) When steam condenses it becomes:
- ☐ ice
- ☐ evaporation
- ☐ liquid water
- ☐ gas

c) When ice melts it becomes:
- ☐ steam
- ☐ liquid water
- ☐ gas
- ☐ solid

d) When water freezes it becomes:
- ☐ melted
- ☐ ice
- ☐ steam
- ☐ liquid

Round Four

a) Water is:
- ☐ a solution
- ☐ a solute
- ☐ a solvent
- ☐ insoluble

b) When a solid mixes completely with a liquid it has:
- ☐ evaporated
- ☐ crystallised
- ☐ condensed
- ☐ dissolved

c) A solid that does not dissolve is:
- ☐ evaporated
- ☐ crystallised
- ☐ insoluble
- ☐ condensed

d) A mixture of salt and water can be separated using:
- ☐ filtration
- ☐ evaporation
- ☐ condensation
- ☐ freezing

Colour in your score here:

☆ ☆ ☆ ☆ ☆ ☆ ☆ ☆ ☆ ☆ ☆

Parents Start Here...

Top Tip! Go through this page as often as you like until your child understands it fully.

It is best to leave experiments with electricity to the school, where they will have the right equipment. Talk to your child about what life must have been like without electricity (and still is, for many millions of children around the world).

Introducing Electricity

We use electricity all of the time.

Most of our electricity comes from the mains. Mains electricity is generated (made) in power stations far away from our homes and it travels through cables and wires.

We plug electrical appliances into the mains sockets.

Mains electricity is extremely powerful and dangerous.
- Never poke things into electrical sockets.
- Water conducts electricity so you must never touch a light switch, plug or socket with wet hands.

Some electrical appliances can get enough electricity from batteries.

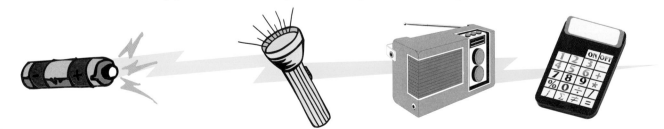

Batteries do not store electricity. They have chemicals inside which react together to make electricity.

Batteries can leak dangerous chemicals so take care with them. Rechargeable batteries can burn you. Never put batteries into a fire. Some batteries can be recycled.

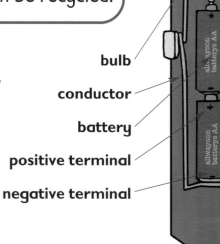

Switch a torch on:

- Electricity flows from the positive terminal, through metal conductors, to the bulb.
- The electricity flows through the very thin wire (also a conductor) in the bulb, making it light up.
- It flows through more metal conductors and back to the negative terminal.

bulb

conductor

battery

positive terminal

negative terminal

Home Learn

1. Mains electricity travels along wires. Are these wires made of:
   - ☐ a) wool
   - ☐ b) metal
   - ☐ c) spaghetti

2. The electrical wires are covered in an electrical insulator. Is it:
   - ☐ a) metal
   - ☐ b) plastic
   - ☐ c) glass

TRY THIS # Activity

If you have use of a computer at home, ask a grown-up to help you research the subject of electricity on the Internet. Alternatively, visit your local library.

Check Your Progress!
Introducing Electricity ☐
Turn to page 48 and put a tick next to what you have just learned.

Top Tip! Don't worry if your child does not understand straightaway – children learn at different speeds.

Parents Start Here...

Your child will cover this subject in greater depth at school, where they can reinforce the learning by actually making circuits themselves.

Working With Electrical Circuits

The flow of electricity from a power source, through conductors, and back to the power source is an electrical circuit.

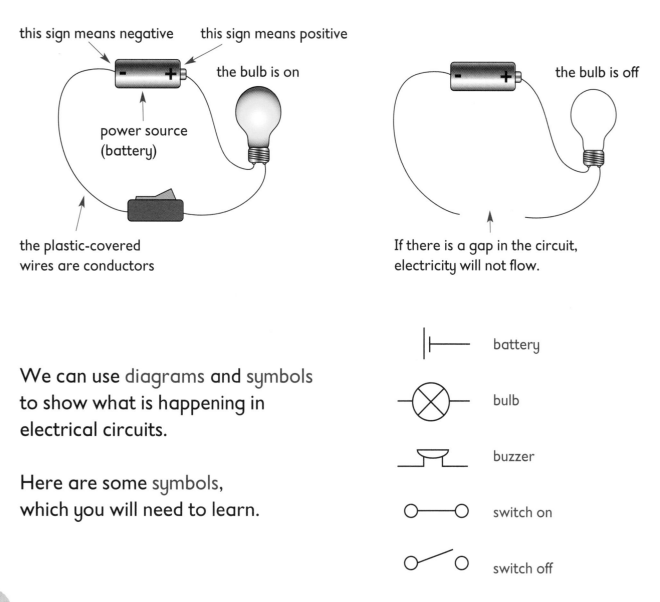

this sign means negative   this sign means positive

the bulb is on

power source (battery)

the plastic-covered wires are conductors

the bulb is off

If there is a gap in the circuit, electricity will not flow.

battery

bulb

buzzer

switch on

switch off

We can use diagrams and symbols to show what is happening in electrical circuits.

Here are some symbols, which you will need to learn.

Here is a simple circuit that is drawn and shown as a diagram:

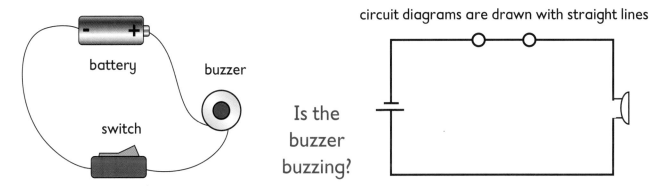

circuit diagrams are drawn with straight lines

battery

buzzer

switch

Is the buzzer buzzing?

Circuits won't work if:
- the battery is flat
- there is a gap in the circuit
- both wires are connected to the same end of the battery.

Home Learn

Are the light bulbs on?

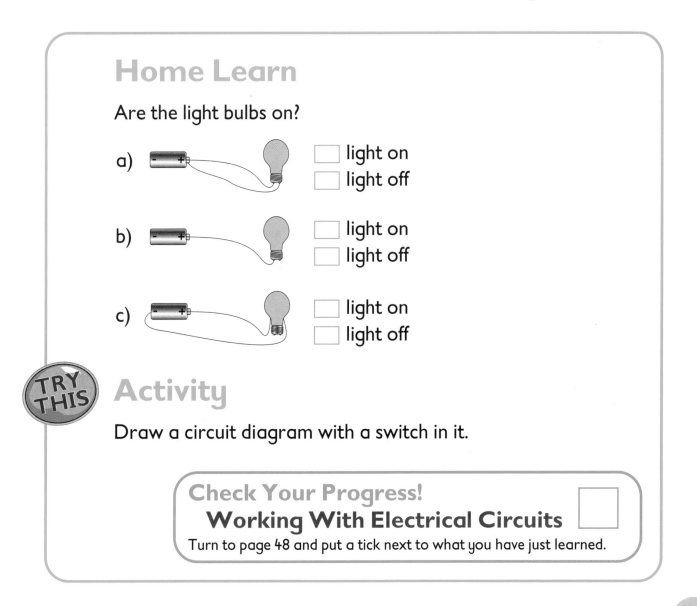

a) ☐ light on
☐ light off

b) ☐ light on
☐ light off

c) ☐ light on
☐ light off

TRY THIS ## Activity

Draw a circuit diagram with a switch in it.

Check Your Progress!
Working With Electrical Circuits
Turn to page 48 and put a tick next to what you have just learned.

Parents Start Here...

Show your child how balanced forces result in no movement. Give examples, like a tug of war or an arm wrestle.

Forces

- Forces either push or pull.
- Forces have a size and a direction. We show these using arrows.

PULL

The arrow shows the size and direction of force.

PUSH

The elephant is using a greater force, so he is more likely to move the crate than the man.

PUSH

Forces can help each other.

PUSH PUSH

Forces work against each other.

Some forces change the shape of things.

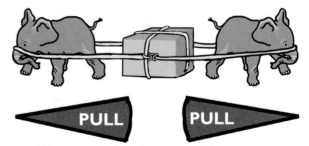

PULL PULL

If two opposing forces are the same size, an object will stay where it is.

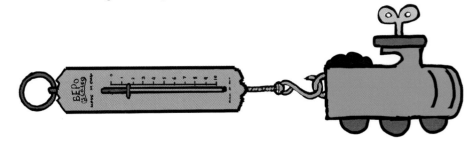

Some forces can be measured using a spring balance or Newton Meter. (Isaac Newton was the scientist who discovered the force of gravity.) It looks a bit like a weighing scale, but the scale is measuring Newtons (unit of force) not grams or kilograms (units of mass or weight), and you can use it sideways or upside down.

Home Learn

Which way do you think the ball will move? Put a tick in the box you think the ball will move towards. Put a tick in both boxes if you think the ball will stay in the same place.

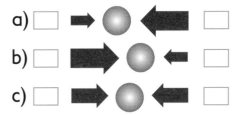

Activity

Sit on the opposite side of a table from a friend. Place a frozen pea in the middle of the table. Use straws to try and blow the peas off the other side of the table. (You can turn this into a game of table football with a little imagination.)

Check Your Progress!

Forces

Turn to page 48 and put a tick next to what you have just learned.

27

Parents Start Here...

Talk about how vehicles are designed to balance their functionality with the need to reduce air or water resistance.

Types Of Forces

Thrust

* The type of force that makes something move is called thrust.
* You need energy to produce thrust. Energy for thrust can come from burning fuel in an engine, or from food.

Friction

* One force that slows things down is friction. Which bicycle, do you think, is travelling faster?

* The rough surface slows the bicycle down. This is because of friction.

* Friction is a force that works against forward thrust. There is always friction when two surfaces move against each other.

Friction can be useful:

Some surfaces have a small amount of friction:

Some have lots of friction:

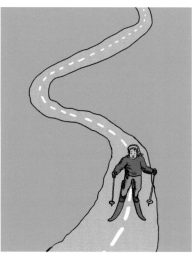

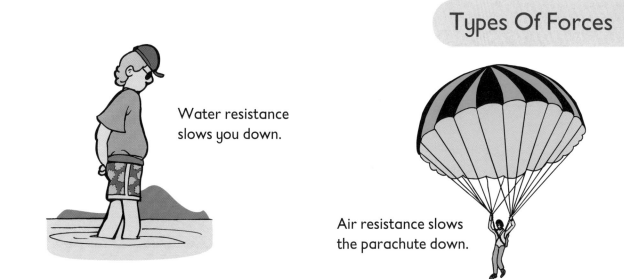

Water resistance slows you down.

Air resistance slows the parachute down.

Air and Water Resistance

- Two more forces that slow things down are air resistance and water resistance.

- You can feel water pushing against you when you try to walk through water. Air resistance is similar, but not nearly so strong.

- Vehicles are designed to be streamlined. This means they are the best shape for moving through water or air.

Home Learn

Tick the objects that are streamlined:

TRY THIS

Activity

Try rubbing the palms of your hands together, fast. You will be able to feel heat being made because of friction. Try the experiment again but coat your hands in soap, oil or butter first. This acts as a lubricant, and reduces friction.

Check Your Progress!
Types Of Forces
Turn to page 48 and put a tick next to what you have just learned.

29

Parents Start Here...

The topic of 'upthrust' has been removed from the National Curriculum. However, a basic understanding of this force helps make more sense of other forces, such as gravity.

Gravity, Upthrust And Magnetism

Gravity

Put this book down, stand up and jump, then sit down again.
You bent your legs and thrust your body upwards to jump up.
But what made you come down again?

- Gravity is a force that keeps all of us on the planet. Without it, we'd be shooting off into space.
- We have gravity because the Earth is a big spinning ball. Big objects attract things to themselves – this is what we call gravity.
- Earth's gravity pulls everything towards the centre of the planet. That's why people in Australia don't fall off!
- The moon is smaller than the Earth, that's why there is less gravity there.
- Deep in space there is no gravity. Things just float about.

Upthrust

If you are swimming, what stops gravity from pulling you to the bottom of the pool?

- Upthrust is the force that pushes up in water or air. When the force of gravity is the same as the force of upthrust, things float.

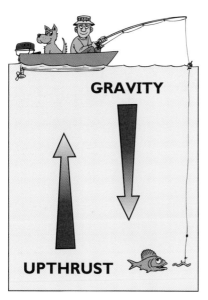

GRAVITY

UPTHRUST

Magnets

- Magnets exert a force on each other. This is magnetic force.
- Magnets have two poles, north and south.

Same poles repel each other:

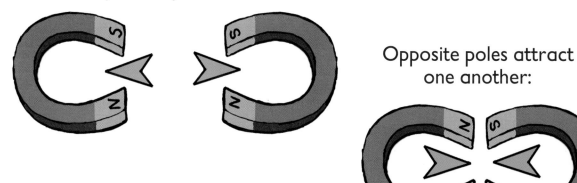

Opposite poles attract one another:

Home Learn

a) Name the force that keeps you on the planet.

_____

b) Name the force that stops a boat from sinking.

_____

c) Name the force between two magnets.

_____

Activity

Experiment with magnets. (You might have some on your fridge.) Never put magnets near electrical equipment, like a television or computer, because they can cause damage.

Check Your Progress!
Gravity, Upthrust And Magnetism
Turn to page 48 and put a tick next to what you have just learned.

Quiz

On Your Marks. In each round, award yourself marks for correct answers. You are allowed to look back through the book for some help.

For ★ ★ ★ get all 4 answers right

For ★ ★ get 3 answers right

For ★ get 1 or 2 answers right

Colour in your total star score at the end of the quiz.

Round One

a) Electricity flows through:
- [ ] conductors
- [ ] insulators
- [ ] decorators
- [ ] perambulators

b) A round flow of electricity is called a:
- [ ] circle
- [ ] circus
- [ ] circumference
- [ ] circuit

c) The symbol ⊢— means:
- [ ] buzzer
- [ ] battery
- [ ] light
- [ ] switch

d) The kettle uses electricity from the:
- [ ] mens
- [ ] means
- [ ] moons
- [ ] mains

Round Two

a) A force can be push or:
- [ ] pulley
- [ ] pounce
- [ ] pullover
- [ ] pull

b) The scientist who discovered gravity was:
- [ ] Thomas Edison
- [ ] Marie Curie
- [ ] Isaac Newton
- [ ] Galileo Galilei

c) The force that requires energy to make things move is:
- ☐ thrust
- ☐ friction
- ☐ wind resistance
- ☐ upthrust

d) The force you can feel when you rub your hands together is:
- ☐ upthrust
- ☐ friction
- ☐ wind resistance
- ☐ thrust

Round Three

a) Electric wires are covered in plastic because plastic is a good:
- ☐ thermal conductor
- ☐ thermal insulator
- ☐ electrical conductor
- ☐ electrical insulator

b) This symbol —⊗— means:
- ☐ battery
- ☐ switch
- ☐ light bulb
- ☐ buzzer

c) This symbol o——o means:
- ☐ battery
- ☐ switch
- ☐ light bulb
- ☐ buzzer

d) The sign + on batteries means:
- ☐ negative
- ☐ positive
- ☐ plus
- ☐ add

Round Four

a) The force that keeps us on the ground is:
- ☐ friction
- ☐ gravity
- ☐ upthrust
- ☐ air resistance

b) The force that slows a parachute down is:
- ☐ friction
- ☐ gravity
- ☐ upthrust
- ☐ air resistance

c) A car that has been designed to reduce air resistance is:
- ☐ rigid
- ☐ durable
- ☐ flexible
- ☐ streamlined

d) There is no gravity:
- ☐ on Earth
- ☐ on the Moon
- ☐ in space
- ☐ on Jupiter

Colour in your score here:

☆ ☆ ☆ ☆ ☆ ☆ ☆ ☆ ☆ ☆

Top Tip!
Learning is fun, so if your child is tired, let them come back to this when they are fresh.

Parents Start Here...

You can expand this topic further. Talk about how light is made of seven constituent colours that get split by prisms, or rain, to produce the seven colours of the rainbow.

Light

Things that give out light are called light sources. If you look out of a window during the day you will see light coming from the Sun.

Never look directly at the Sun. It can blind you.

the Sun is a light source

electric lights are a source of light

You have electric lights in your home and at school.

Light sources also produce heat. Do not touch lights – you might get burnt. Do not let anything touch a light bulb – it might catch fire.

On bonfire night you will see light coming from fires and fireworks.

these are also sources of light

Candles, computers and televisions are sources of light.

Some things look like light, but they are just reflecting light that is around them. Smooth or shiny objects reflect light best. The Moon may look bright, but it just reflects light that comes from the Sun.

Things you should know about light:

- Light travels in straight lines (rays).
- If something blocks a ray of light a shadow is cast.
- Light travels very fast: 300 million metres every second. This is known as the speed of light.

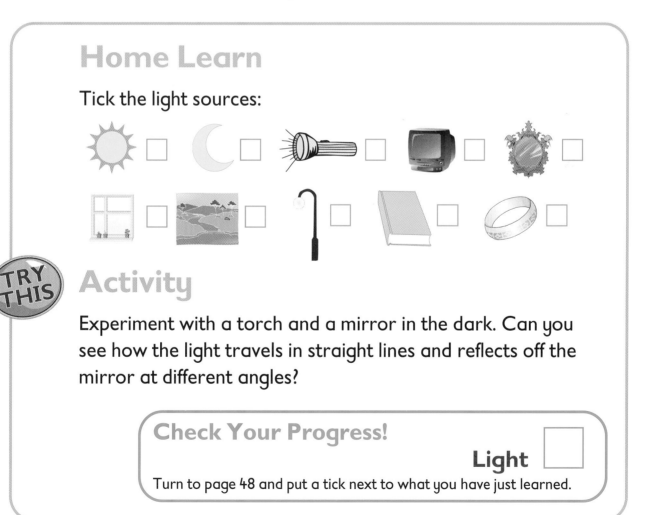

Home Learn

Tick the light sources:

TRY THIS Activity

Experiment with a torch and a mirror in the dark. Can you see how the light travels in straight lines and reflects off the mirror at different angles?

Check Your Progress!

Light

Turn to page 48 and put a tick next to what you have just learned.

Parents Start Here...

Point out your child's shadow to them at different times of day.

Reflection And Shadows

Reflection

Stand in front of a mirror in a dark room.

Shine a torch at the mirror: Now point the torch from one side:

The light shines right back at you.

The light bounces off the mirror and reflects to the other side.

Mirrors reflect light. This is possible because light travels in straight lines.

- Everything around you (unless it is completely black) is reflecting light.
- This light then reaches your eyes.
- Your eyes pass a message to your brain, telling it about the light.
- Your brain turns these messages into vision.

This is how you see.

Shadows

When a person or an object is in the Sun, it makes a shadow. This is because your it is blocking the Sun's rays.

When the sun is high in the sky (midday) your shadow will be smaller. When the sun is low in the sky (morning and evening) your shadow will be longer.

Home Learn

How do we see a tree? Tick the correct box.

☐ a) Moon ➡ tree ➡ eye

☐ b) Sun ➡ eye ➡ tree

☐ c) Sun ➡ tree ➡ eye

Activity

Use a torch in a darkened room to create shadows on the walls. Use your hands to make a shadow crocodile and duck.

Check Your Progress!
Reflection And Shadows ☐

Turn to page 48 and put a tick next to what you have just learned.

Parents Start Here...

Top Tip!
Go through this page as often as you like until your child understands it fully.

Set up a series of glass bottles with differing amounts of water and show your child how to blow across the top to produce sound.

Sound

We know that things are made from tiny particles. (Look back at page 10 to remind yourself, if necessary.)

- When particles are disturbed they vibrate. This means they jiggle around very quickly.
- When these particles vibrate they make the particles in the air around them vibrate too.
- This vibration causes sound.

Sound travels in waves like this:

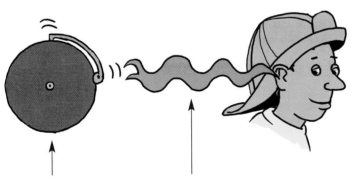

OBJECT VIBRATES   **AIR VIBRATES**

The sound travels to our ears. Our eardrums vibrate and send the message about the sound to our brain, which then hears the noise.

If the disturbance of particles is big, the sound is loud.
If the disturbance of particles is small, the sound is quiet.

- Sound can travel through water. You may have noticed that you can't hear things very well underwater. That is because sound does not travel as well in water as it does in air.

- Sound can travel through objects, but it passes through some objects, such as wood, better than others, e.g. a pillow.

Put your ear on one end of a wooden table and ask someone to tap their fingers on the other end. You will find the sound is louder than you would expect.

Pitch

The pitch of a sound is how low or high it is. When we play musical instruments we talk about the sound they make in terms of pitch and note.

This violin has strings. When the strings are played they vibrate, creating sound. The shorter the string, the higher the note is.

Tight strings will also give higher notes.

Home Learn

a) We hear sound using our ears, our ear drums and our kidneys. ☐ True ☐ False
b) Sound is caused by the vibration of particles in objects. ☐ True ☐ False
c) A short guitar string, when plucked, makes a lower note than a long guitar string. ☐ True ☐ False

Activity

Make a telephone using two empty yoghurt cartons and a long piece of string. You will discover the string needs to be taut for sound to travel.

Check Your Progress!

Sound ☐

Turn to page 48 and put a tick next to what you have just learned.

Parents Start Here...

Helping your child research a topic like leap years, will enable them to develop research skills.

Days And Years

we are here

- We have day and night because the Earth spins.

During The Night:
The Earth has spun around so that the side we're on is in the dark. When it is night time for us, it is daytime in Australia.

During The Day:
The Earth has spun around so that the side we're on is in the light. When it is daytime for us, it is night time in Australia.

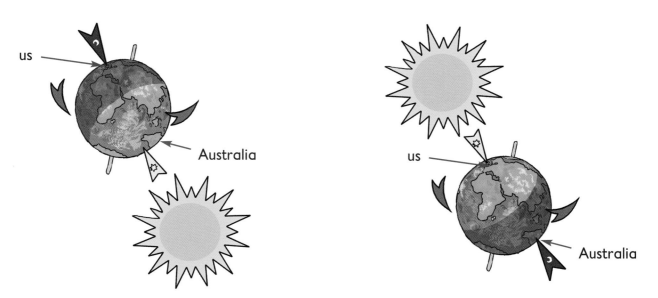

us → ← Australia

us → ← Australia

- It takes 24 hours for the Earth to spin all of the way around, so a day is 24 hours long. (We use the word 'day' to mean daytime as well as 24 hours — it can be confusing.)
- For tens of thousands of years people believed that the Sun moved across the sky, because that's what it looks like.

- But now we know, because of brilliant scientists like Copernicus and Galileo, that the Earth moves around the Sun, not the other way round.
- It takes $365\frac{1}{4}$ days for the Earth to move around the Sun. The journey around the Sun is called the Earth's orbit.
- The Earth spins on its axis.

Make your own Earth to see what this means:
1. You need an orange, a sharp stick, a pen, a lamp and a grown-up.
2. Ask the grown-up to push the stick through the orange from top to bottom and draw a blob to show where we are.

Begin to spin the orange on its axis. As it turns you will see how we are in dark, light and then dark again. You can see how countries that lie on the equator (across the belly of the orange) are closer to the Sun than us. That's why they are hotter.

tip the orange slightly

North Pole

the stick shows the Earth's axis

me

South Pole

Home Learn

a) The Earth spins on its axis once a year. ☐ True ☐ False
b) The Sun travels around the Earth every $365\frac{1}{4}$ years.
☐ True ☐ False
c) We have 24 hours of daylight. ☐ True ☐ False

TRY THIS

Activity

Try spinning your orange Earth around the lamp, so you can see how the Earth turns on its axis while also spinning in an orbit around the Sun.

Check Your Progress!
Days And Years
Turn to page 48 and put a tick next to what you have just learned.

Parents Start Here...

Top Tip! If your child loses concentration here, let them take a break.

Children love the idea of space, planets and stars. There are lots of facts and figures for them to learn and ideas to engage their imaginations. Use star charts to help your child identify the celestial bodies in the night sky.

Our Planet And Its Neighbours

The Moon
- The Moon orbits the Earth once every 28 days.
- Our calendar is based on the Moon's orbit.
- The Moon exerts a gravitational force on the Earth that causes waves and tides.
- The Moon is not a light source; it reflects light from the Sun.
- When the Moon is in the Earth's shadow, we can only see part of it.

The Earth is just one of nine planets (that we know about) orbiting the Sun. The Sun and the planets that orbit it are called our Solar System.

Jupiter is the largest planet in our Solar System. It is made of a mixture of rock, liquid and gases and has 16 moons. It takes nearly 12 Earth years for Jupiter to orbit the Sun.

Venus is the hottest planet in our Solar System; even hotter than Mercury, which is closer to the Sun. Temperatures can reach 480°C. One day on Venus lasts 243 Earth days.

We know about the planets in our Solar System because of powerful telescopes on Earth and in space, like the Hubble Space Telescope.

Our Solar System is part of the Milky Way Galaxy. There are estimated to be over 100 billion stars in the Milky Way. Some people say that there are so many billions and billions of planets in the Universe that life must exist on at least one more of them. What do you think?

Do you know the difference between a planet and a star?
A star is a light source. Light is produced from gases that continually explode like massive bombs. Planets do not produce light, they only reflect it. Our Sun is a star, the Earth is a planet.

Home Learn

Complete the sentences using these words:

**Saturn   spins   Jupiter   orbits
Man United   hits   Venus   Milky Way**

a) The moon _____ the Earth every 28 days.

b) Planet _____ is the largest in our Solar System.

c) Our galaxy is called the _____ _____ .

TRY THIS Activity

Find out some more about the Hubble Space Telescope.

Check Your Progress!
Our Planet And Its Neighbours
Turn to page 48 and put a tick next to what you have just learned.

Quiz

On Your Marks. In each round, award yourself marks for correct answers. You are allowed to look back through the book for some help.

For ⭐ ⭐ ⭐ get all 4 answers right

For ⭐ ⭐ get 3 answers right

For ⭐ get 1 or 2 answers right

Colour in your total star score at the end of the quiz.

Round One

a) Tick the light source:
- ☐ Sun
- ☐ Moon
- ☐ Earth
- ☐ Jupiter

b) Tick the light source:
- ☐ picture
- ☐ mirror
- ☐ television
- ☐ book

c) Tick the light source:
- ☐ lamp
- ☐ lampshade
- ☐ plug
- ☐ silver

d) Tick the light source:
- ☐ wood
- ☐ fire
- ☐ window
- ☐ kettle

Round Two

a) The speed of light is:
- ☐ 300 million metres per second
- ☐ 30 metres per second
- ☐ 3 million metres per second
- ☐ 3 metres per second

b) At 1 pm your shadow would be:
- ☐ absent
- ☐ long
- ☐ short
- ☐ everywhere

c) Light travels in:
- ☐ wavy lines
- ☐ straight lines
- ☐ curves
- ☐ light bulbs

d) Sound is caused by:
- ☐ multiplication
- ☐ amplification
- ☐ vibration
- ☐ hibernation

Round Three

a) The Earth spins on its axis once every:
- ☐ 24 hours
- ☐ 60 minutes
- ☐ 28 days
- ☐ 365 ¼ days

b) The moon orbits the Earth once every:
- ☐ 24 hours
- ☐ 60 minutes
- ☐ 28 days
- ☐ 365 ¼ days

c) The Earth orbits the Sun once every:
- ☐ 24 hours
- ☐ 60 minutes
- ☐ 28 days
- ☐ 365 ¼ days

d) Copernicus and Galileo are:
- ☐ moons of Jupiter
- ☐ scientists
- ☐ planets
- ☐ solar systems

Round Four

a) The planet closest to the Sun is:
- ☐ Earth
- ☐ Mercury
- ☐ Venus
- ☐ Pluto

b) The hottest planet in our solar system is:
- ☐ Uranus
- ☐ Mercury
- ☐ Venus
- ☐ Pluto

c) The biggest planet in our solar system is:
- ☐ Earth
- ☐ Mercury
- ☐ Venus
- ☐ Jupiter

d) Our galaxy is called:
- ☐ Solar System
- ☐ Earth
- ☐ Milky Way
- ☐ Universe

Colour in your score here:

☆ ☆ ☆ ☆ ☆ ☆ ☆ ☆ ☆ ☆ ☆

Word Search

```
j   n   e   p   t   u   n   e   e   t   m

u   u   m   i   l   k   y   w   a   y   e

r   y   p   m   a   r   s   e   r   h   r

a   v   s   i   a   p   a   i   t   w   c

n   r   u   m   t   y   t   l   h   a   u

u   n   z   o   s   e   u   t   g   k   r

s   a   q   o   h   o   r   b   i   t   y

t   e   r   n   c   h   n   i   e   s   b

p   l   u   t   o   y   v   e   n   u   s

g   a   l   i   l   e   o   s   p   n   p
```

Find the words:

Sun   Mercury   Venus   Earth   Moon   Mars
Jupiter   Saturn   Uranus   Neptune   Pluto

Find the mystery words:
a) A journey around a planet or star
b) Our galaxy
c) A famous scientist

Answers

Page 5:
Home Learn
a) Glass is hard, rigid, transparent, waterproof and smooth.
b) A plastic raincoat is soft, flexible, opaque, waterproof and smooth.
c) A nappy is soft, flexible, opaque, absorbent and smooth.

Page 7:
Home Learn
a) Hammers are always made with metal heads. The handles can be wood, rubber or plastic.
b) Cars can contain wood, metal, plastic, glass, leather and fabric.
c) Transparent plastic is used in tableware, water bottles, food packaging, conservatory roofs, document folders, credit card holders; lots of places!

Page 9:
Home Learn
1. Stirring a hot sauce with a wooden spoon is a good idea because wood is a thermal insulator.
2. Stirring a hot sauce with a metal spoon is a bad idea because metal is a thermal conductor.

Page 11:
Home Learn

	Solid	Liquid	Gas
Vinegar		✓	
Oxygen			✓
Petrol		✓	
Jelly	✓		
Plastic	✓		
Mercury		✓	
Carbon Dioxide			✓
Paper	✓		
Blood		✓	
Helium			✓

Page 13:
Home Learn
When water is cooled it evaporates. False
The particles in steam are further apart than the particles in water. True
Rain is melted snow falling from the clouds. False
Ice floats because water expands when it freezes. True

Page 15:
Home Learn
a) When a solid does not dissolve in water we say it is insoluble.
b) Water dissolves some solids so we say it is a solvent.

Page 17:
Home Learn

	Reversible	Irreversible
Freezing a chicken	✓	
Boiling an egg		✓
Dissolving sugar in water	✓	
Baking bread		✓
Melting candle wax	✓	
Grilling bread to make toast		✓

Page 19:
Home Learn
You would separate sand and water using filtration: pour the mixture through a filter paper and the sand would be trapped while the water passes through.

Pages 20–21:
Quiz
Round One
a) Wool
b) Metal
c) Polythene
d) Stainless steel

Round Two
a) Helium
b) Oil
c) Coal
d) Water

Round Three
a) Water vapour
b) Liquid water
c) Liquid water
d) Ice

Round Four
a) A solvent
b) Dissolved
c) Insoluble
d) Evaporation

Page 23:
Home Learn
1. Metal
2. Plastic

Page 25:
Home Learn
a) The light will not come on because both the wires are connected to the same end of the battery.
b) The light will not come on because the circuit is not complete; there is no wire from the bulb to the battery.
c) The light bulb will come on.

Page 27:
Home Learn
a) The ball will move towards the box on the left.
b) The ball will move towards box on the right.
c) The ball does not move; the forces are balanced.

Page 29:
Home Learn
The fish, electric train, Formula One car and swallow are all streamlined.

Page 31:
Home Learn
a) Gravity
b) Upthrust
c) Magnetism

Pages 32–33:
Quiz
Round One
a) Conductors
b) Circuit
c) Battery
d) Mains

Round Two
a) Pull
b) Isaac Newton
c) Thrust
d) Friction

Round Three
a) Electrical insulator
b) Light bulb
c) Switch
d) Positive

Round Four
a) Gravity
b) Air resistance
c) Streamlined
d) In space

Page 35:
Home Learn
The Sun, television, street lamp and torch are all light sources.

Page 37:
Home Learn
(c) is the correct answer.

Page 39:
Home Learn
a) We hear sound using our ears, our ear drums and our kidneys. False
b) Sound is caused by the vibration of particles in objects. True
c) A short guitar string, when plucked, makes a lower note than a long guitar string. False

Page 41:
Home Learn
a) The Earth spins on its axis once a year. False
b) The Sun travels around the Earth every 365¼ years. False
c) We have 24 hours of daylight. False

Page 43:
Home Learn
a) The moon orbits the Earth every 28 days.
b) Planet Jupiter is the largest in our Solar System.
c) Our galaxy is called the Milky Way.

Pages 44–45:
Quiz
Round One
a) Sun
b) Television
c) Lamp
d) Fire

Round Two
a) 300 million metres per second
b) Short
c) Straight lines
d) Vibration

Round Three
a) 24 hours
b) 28 days
c) 365¼ days
d) Scientists

Round Four
a) Mercury
b) Venus
c) Jupiter
d) Milky Way

Page 46:
Word Search

Mystery words:
a) Orbit
b) Milky Way
c) Galileo

Check Your Progress!

Materials.. ☐

Materials And Properties .... ☐

Conductors And Insulators .... ☐

Solids, Liquids And Gases .... ☐

Water .... ☐

Mixing Materials .... ☐

Changing And Changing Back..................................... ☐

Separating .... ☐

Introducing Electricity .... ☐

Working With Electrical Circuits .... ☐

Forces .... ☐

Types Of Force.. ☐

Gravity, Upthrust And Magnetism .... ☐

Light .... ☐

Reflection And Shadows .... ☐

Sound .... ☐

Days And Years .... ☐

Our Planet And Its Neighbours .... ☐